GHOSTLY
OF CORNWALL
FOR THE 21st CENTURY

IAN ADDICOAT

AKASHIC BOOKS

23 Pendennis Road,
Penzance,
Cornwall TR18 2BA

Tel:
01736 331206

GHOSTLY TALES OF CORNWALL
For the 21st Century

IAN ADDICOAT (Bsc, Hons)

COPYRIGHT IM ADDICOAT, 2001

Published by: Akashic Books
23 Pendennis Road, Penzance, TR18 2BA

Printed and bound in the UK

ISBN 0-9538274-1-0

Also visit www.ghosthunting.org.uk

Front cover: Pengersick Castle, Praa Sands, Cornwall.
"the most haunted location in the UK"?
photograph taken and kindly provided by Geoff Buswell.

Contents

Introduction: "Ghosts in Cornwall"

Pengersick Castle	Praa Sands	1
Marazion Ghosts	Marazion	5
Kenegie	Gulval	6
Chapel Street	Penzance	9
Humphry Davy's Ghost?	Penzance	11
Market Jew Street	Penzance	12
Ghostly Footsteps	Penzance	13
The Bread Street Gypsy	Penzance	15
The Old Ones	Mousehole	17
Mysterious Monks	Newlyn	21
The Fishermen Ghosts	Newlyn/ Hayle	22
Bodriggy House	Hayle	24
Skidden Hill	St Ives	26
Mysterious Lands End/ Castle Carn Brea/ Porthcurno/ Sennen	Lands End	28
The Miners	Carnyorth/ Levant	31
Truro Ghosts	Truro	32
Bodmin Moor	Bodmin	34
Lanhydrock House	Bodmin	37
Bodmin Gaol	Bodmin	38
The Lost Gardens of Heligan	St Austell	39
Roche Rock	St Austell	40
Previous Book Updates		41

ACKNOWLEDGMENTS

I apologise for what will no doubt be deemed a boring acknowledgments page but I would genuinely like to thank a great number of people for their assistance during the creation of this book and for other help and guidance. Unfortunately I cannot name them all!

I would like to thank all the people who contributed their time and precious stories to me. I am forever grateful to those who have willingly shared their personal experiences and knowledge with me. There are too many to name but that does not diminish my gratitude.

I am also grateful to all of the organisations and locations who allowed me access to information and a chance to do some research or helped me in other ways.

I also give special thanks to: The Cornishman Newspaper; The Ghost Club Society; Radio Cornwall; Pirate FM; Golowan; Geoff Buswell; Max Channon; Angela Evans; my parents, my friends and many more besides.

But most of all, more than anyone else: my wife Debbie, daughter Alishia and son Connor, for their patience, help, support and especially love.

INTRODUCTION

GHOSTS IN CORNWALL

Many people believe that ghosts are "just a trick of the mind", "hallucinations"; "caused by drunkenness", or perhaps the result of large scale "trickery", "liars" and "pranksters". On the other hand, there are just as many people who believe that ghosts are "very real", "proving life after death", and that a "consciousness transcends death". There are even people who believe that ghosts are "time travellers", or "aliens from another dimension", but I won't get too far into that!

The truth is that nobody is able to offer conclusive proof one way or another. "One man's ghost is another man's crumpet" (or something like that!). Nevertheless, the subject continues to fascinate millions around the world. Like it or not! ghosts are here to stay! Studies show that vast proportions of people claim to see ghosts (perhaps 1 in 5). Throughout history and across all civilisations, ghosts have reared their ugly heads. Beyond the fantastical tales, there are countless stories which are very convincing.

However, here in Cornwall ghosts are even more common, it is not described as "the most haunted county in England", for nothing. Even as far away as Eastern Europe, they start their ghost stories with the words: "once upon a time in a castle in Cornwall...". Whether or not you believe in ghosts, it is difficult not to acknowledge their place in Cornish culture and legend. Every town and village has it's own tales of ghosts, mysterious phantoms and hauntings. No place on earth has as much to tell about ghostly phenomenon.

Can it be just dismissed as a symptom of a superstitious people? A deeply Celtic heritage? the absorbing history? the brooding ancient stones and monuments? the plentiful granite? the abundant Ley lines? or even the weather? All of these things have been used to explain Cornwall's ghostly heritage but never seem to fulfil peoples desire for answers. Perhaps

Cornwall simply has more than it's fair share of ghosts. With the mysterious atmosphere; brooding countryside; hostile sea; rugged coastlines; historic traditions; sense of tragedy and fascinating people, why shouldn't it? One look at Cornwall's rich tapestry of legend and history is spellbinding. You would almost be disappointed if you were not to find a ghostly story creeping around every corner.

Perhaps you yourself may be lucky enough (or unlucky enough!) to have a similar encounter. Remember, though, that whatever you believe ghosts to be: whether a projection out of the past; a hallucination, caused by the brain; or a lost soul, stuck between this world and the next, you may wish to be thoughtful. After all, if they are a former person, now deceased, they may have feelings! so please treat them, as you would wish to be treated, be kind, considerate and respectful, just in case!

Please note: The main desire of this book is to bring these stories to your attention and to the attention of those in the future. Otherwise many such tales will simply be forgotten. The stories appearing in this book are completely genuine as told or researched by me. On a few occasions names have been altered to assure anonymity. Otherwise details have stayed as true as possible to the original accounts. Unfortunately, it is never possible to guarantee the complete accuracy of stories of this nature but the author assures you he has taken every possible step to maintain credibility and accuracy. Where possible each story has been verified by a number of witnesses and cross matched with other accounts. Historical documents; plans; and literature have been consulted where available. No liberties were taken and the benefit of the doubt was never assumed. Therefore the reader can rest assured that every step possible has been taken to make these stories as accurate and truthful as possible.

If you have a 'ghostly' story to share or more information about the tales in this book, I would be delighted to hear from you. Please write c/o the publishers address, at the front. Thank you.

PENGERSICK CASTLE, PRAA SANDS

"There is no doubt that this building is the most haunted location in the U.K. at this time " The Ghost Club Society, January, 2001.

For the oldest investigation group in the world to make such a statement, you have to take notice. Many buildings in the country lay claims to such a title, yet none can claim such an endorsement as Pengersick Castle. So what is it about this Medieval tower which causes such assertions?

The fortified tower was originally believed to be part of a Twelfth Century manor house, rebuilt and strengthened in Tudor times by John Milliton. Stories and legends abound about the castle: tales of black magic, sword and sorcery, witches, smuggling, murder, mystery and above all ghosts. It is difficult to separate fact from fiction (although a vast amount of information has been published elsewhere). Nevertheless, there seems little doubt that a ghostly heritage remains today.

Many different people have claimed to see the many ghosts which manifest themselves in the tower and the surrounding grounds. These include a wandering monk; a wise woman; misty like forms; Lady Engrina Pengersick; a knight; a re-enactment of a murder; John Milliton; strange, eerie lights; a demon hound; and many others besides (indeed over twenty separate presences). Interestingly, many of these do fit the sordid history and the misfortunes of the Milliton and Pengersick families.

A medieval rape and murder has apparently been re-enacted in front of several stunned witnesses, including members of a Ghost Club investigation team. Many people have claimed to have seen a ghostly monk walking through a wall or wandering around in the castle grounds. At times "sensitive people", have claimed to have spoken to the spirit of the monk, who has apparently confessed to certain misdeeds. He is said to be a burly monk, wearing a black robe and wide brimmed hat, from the 14th century. A nurse or wise woman has been seen in the haunted bedroom standing next to the Medieval bed and another lady, Engrina Pengersick? has been seen in the room and on the bed itself. The figure of a man has also been seen standing in the corner of the room, this is believed to be either a knight, Henry Le Fort Pengersick or even John Milliton. Talking of John Milliton, there is also a bizarre claim that a demon is present in the room. During one of his occult sessions, John Milliton is said to have conjured up this demon, which has remained there to this day, preying on peoples fear. Personally, I confess to being just a little sceptical about this! However, people do claim that this resident of hell resides in the fireplace and appears in the form of a black, ominous mist or as glowing red eyes in the shape of a dog. Demon or not, several people have certainly witnessed a peculiar, terrifying misty form, slowly floating across the bedroom at floor level.

The mysterious occurrences in this eerie room are countless. People feel the room pulsing "as though alive", there is a charged atmosphere and a feeling of malevolence. Many people flee from the room from fear or feel physically drained. Several years ago a German lady stayed in the bedroom over night. She left very abruptly and never returned again. Another lady was so overcome, she left amid claims that she found it: "the most evil place she had ever been". Electrical malfunctions are countless and the strange lights and shadowy shapes appear all too frequently. On many occasions investigators of the Ghost Club have witnessed and recorded strange phenomena. Numerous local people and sceptical visitors have themselves witnessed supernatural goings on in the bedroom. However, there are numerous other figures: a woman who was stabbed to death in the 15th century appears at the spot of her murder; a man stabbed and strangled in the 16th century appears by the fireplace; a thirteen year old girl who once danced right off the battlements is said to make her presence felt, trying to dance with people leading them to the battlements; a four year old boy often tugs at women's dresses; and there are others besides. Last year an Australian film crew, accompanied by Channel 5 attempted to capture a ghost on film and local Carlton TV found their equipment mysteriously failing during filming; Sky television also filmed for a whole week here, such is the reputation of the place.

Figures have been seen at Pengersick Castle by numerous reliable witnesses, many people have felt those familiar chills and a sudden, icy drop in temperature. Others have felt a terrifyingly uncomfortable presence and fled the building. On countless occasions people have seen energy lights dancing across the room and on top of the bed. These are often linked to manifestations and appear at the time of a ghostly apparition. Like particles of exploding dust these are said to be caused by an electrical charge, perhaps created by a ghost. Can so many witnesses all be wrong? If we can believe just half of them, then it may be little wonder that Pengersick has achieved it's tag as "the most haunted building in the country".

I have now visited Pengersick on countless occasions, including at night and once for a whole night and I have myself, with others, experienced several very strange occurrences. I am someone who has always been initially questioning about ghostly stories. I prefer to be objective and allow my own evidence to be accumulated before I pass judgement. Sometimes this causes consternation but I like to think that if I experience something it is unlikely to be 'imagination' or 'wishful thinking'. If you look for a rational explanation first and are then left with a supernatural one, then the chances are it will be more genuine. As a result of my experiences at Pengersick I have to conclude that there is certainly something very strange about the building.

I first visited properly with the Ghost Club back in April, 2001 and some very interesting things occurred: the haunted bedroom often became unnaturally cold and we witnessed several strange floating lights and a peculiar atmosphere often enveloped the room, forming as if a thunder storm was brewing, electrifying. A control object: a very heavy Celtic cross, moved a small distance when no human hand could have interfered. Cameras and camcorders kept going wrong and batteries drained down in equipment in seconds. Several, more sensitive people, claimed that certain presences appeared and in all it was a very strange night.

I have since visited and experienced other very strange phenomena: I was once present with a medium who went in to trance and seemed to be speaking in tongues as if taken over by firstly the monk and then a far more ancient spirit, with the most peculiar language I had ever heard; peoples electrical equipment has failed on almost every visit; the coldness, the floating lights and the atmospheres, seem to never fail to make an appearance, indeed I have copies of very clear photographs of these mysterious lights; presences are often felt; there are very strong results with dowsing; I have seen shadowy forms; seen lights suddenly go out; and doors open or slam by themselves; watched people become desperately anxious and overcome with emotion; and many other events besides. I also have a copy of a tape recording made in the grounds when a ghostly chant, like a monk singing in Latin appeared, this is very clear and there is no question of tampering or a hoax.
Once, twenty of us clearly saw a series of shadows running around in the grounds at a site of a former dwelling. These were clearly rodents, complete with tails but they were just the shadows, no sign of actual animals. Indeed, this strange phenomenon was even witnessed by Alexander the castle cat, who attempted to catch them and became very confused when he could not. These images were also captured on video film.

I can conclude, without doubt that Pengersick is the most mysterious place I have ever visited! It has a uniquely strange atmosphere. Countless people have claimed to have seen ghosts here, can they all be wrong?

MARAZION

Marazion has many ghostly stories and legends. For example, St Michael's Mount has some very interesting tales (see Ghost Hunting, page 33...).

Marazion green is said to be haunted by a ghostly white lady who used to appear late at night. She would suddenly materialise in front of staggered witnesses and would then walk alongside people for some distance before slowly fading away. This scared a great number of local residents, who refused to venture on to the green at night. Unfortunately, there have not been quite as many sightings in recent years.

Many years ago people also refused to cross Marazion marsh after night fall. This was because people on horse back had often seen a white lady suddenly rise from the ground and jump on to the back of the horse, to ride pillion. It is also said that sightings of her have become very infrequent. Surely, this fall in sightings recently is a testament to modern transport!

There is a house in Marazion with a very ghostly reputation. Many people have had strange experiences: these include strange footsteps, loud noises and seeing things move, always without explanation. On one occasion a couple moved in for a few weeks and had some terrifying experiences themselves. On the first day they moved their belongings in to the house and unpacked a kettle to make a cup of tea. To their astonishment they watched the kettle lift off the floor and slowly float across the room. As the weeks went by things kept happening and eventually they decided to move back out again!

KENEGIE, GULVAL

Near the village of Gulval (near Penzance) lies the Kenegie hotel. Here was the former mediaeval manor house. Much has been written about the property and at times it has been claimed to be "the most haunted building in the country". In truth such claims are impossible to substantiate but without doubt Kenegie has gained an extremely ghostly reputation over the years. The majority of the hauntings relate to the Harris family who owned the property for about two hundred years, until 1775. It seems that many of them weren't too happy about leaving!

Many of the stories can be traced back to the local author William Bottrell writing at the end of the nineteenth century. He first told of the ghost of "Thrifty Old Harris" buried in the family vault in Gulval church yard. This gent loved the house and put a great deal of time and effort into the manor. Therefore, after his death he could not be persuaded to leave and is claimed to appear one night a year to check on his beloved home. He supposedly becomes angered if he sees anything untoward or in disrepair or if the front door is not left open for him. Bottrell also wrote about the ghost of a housekeeper who haunted the house on the night of her funeral and after. She began to walk down the corridor between rooms, banging doors, before entering the kitchen. Once inside, she began to shriek and rattle plates before heading up the stairs to her master's bedroom, where the noises finally stopped. For years afterwards people claimed to be in the kitchen and suddenly feel a "slap" across their face by an unseen hand and many people believed they saw the housekeeper herself in the court yard. Eventually, as the story goes, her spirit was banished to a small, walled up, room where to this day strange noises can still be heard coming from inside the wall.

Another, "Wild Harris", was master, along with his father to the housekeeper above. He was something of a miser who one day was thrown from his horse and died. After his death he continued to be seen in the area on horse back, dressed in his familiar hunting clothes or he was seen standing at the entrance to the manor. It is also claimed that Wild Harris and a dozen or so other spirits would often be heard in the Summer House late at night, shouting and laughing. Later, his beloved dog also died and it was said that from then on Wild Harris would always be seen accompanied by his favourite canine. It is told that several vicars attempted to exorcise him "unsuccessfully", until finally the famed ghost layer Reverend Polkinghorne led him to nearby Castle-an-Dinas, to perform an infinite task.

The final Harris ghost, described by William Bottrell in the Cornishman newspaper between December, 26th 1878 and January, 9th, 1879 was "Old Man Harris". He died, leaving his estate and will unsolved and was later seen by his solicitor on several occasions after his death.

What can we make of these stories? Victorian, Gothic invention? Over exaggerated tales? Factual ghosts, long departed? or is it possible that the Harris ghosts still remain?

Harris or not, cannot be affirmed, but certainly strange occurrences have continued to blight the Kenegie buildings and some of the events do correspond to some of the above tales.

Years ago two guests separately saw a tall woman in a black satin dress in the lounge. She had a waist band with a set of keys hanging from them. However, this woman, described by the two guests identically, was not a member of staff known to the hotel. This is the same room where people have described feeling a strange presence, that seems to be female but disliking of other women. There also used to be a picture hanging on the wall of Elizabeth I which would frequently be tilted on the wall, by itself, with no explanation. Perhaps this is related to the housekeeper, whose ghost was supposedly walled up. Interestingly, I received a phone call from a lady who once stayed at the Kenegie and was repeatedly woken at night by loud banging on the wall in her room, she was very disturbed when she found out in the morning that there was no room on the opposite side of the wall and vowed never to return.

Other strange things have happened elsewhere. For example years ago in the Tudor Bar people saw a man dressed in brown clothes standing next to the fire place, he suddenly vanished.

Voices have often been heard in an empty room from outside as if there are several people having a conversation but on entering nobody is there. In the kitchen, the sounds of laughter have been heard coming from mid air, as if a young lady is giggling to herself. On several occasions light switches have flicked by themselves, taps have been turned on and the cooker switched on, all by themselves. In one of the bedrooms there is claimed to be a "Stroking Ghost". Several women have claimed that they have woken at night to see their door open by itself and suddenly felt a stoking hand brush their face, in what seems to be a comforting manner. It particularly happened during World War II when Land Girls were stationed here but it has also happened several times since. There seems to be no explanation but the ghost seems to be caring rather than hostile.

A few years ago there were a lot of renovations going on at the Kenegie Hotel while a swimming pool was built. At this time the peculiar activities centred around the building were increased substantially. Things seemed to go wild! Perhaps the ghost of Thrifty Old Harris had returned to show his utmost disapproval of the new addition of a swimming pool?

There are other stories relating to the Kenegie Hotel about strange sounds and sightings and the legend of the Cradle. But the final story may relate to an old favourite. Many people have claimed to have been on the drive to Kenegie and suddenly heard the unmistakable sound of horses footsteps and a carriage trundling along. Though on most occasions nothing has appeared. For instance, one New Year's Eve a young man was due to attend a party at Kenegie but was rather late. As he rushed towards the hotel he had a terrifying experience. Just after midnight the guests were surprised by the door flying open and a white faced man running into the room. He soon told of his sighting of a spectral carriage trundling along the driveway. Other's have even claimed to have seen a ghostly carriage parked up by the hotel complete with headless horses. It seems very likely that if this is true, they can only be those from Penzance described in "Ghost Hunting".

CHAPEL STREET, PENZANCE

Chapel street is one of the oldest and most interesting streets in Penzance and it is also probably the most haunted!

It 'oozes' history from every corner and has always been an important street for both business and architecture. Today it's buildings hide many older buildings, dating from the 13th century and all centuries since. However, many of the buildings hide some other intriguing secrets!

It seems that almost every other building in the Chapel Street area houses it's resident ghost, certainly it has more than it's fair share. Is this due to the history? the ley line said to run across it? or the frequency of visitors and the character of residents over the centuries? It is impossible to determine but there is no doubt that it does have a ghostly heritage.

Many readers will have already read about some of the areas ghosts in my last book: The ghosts of nearby Abbey Slip; the infamous Mrs Baines; and the figure of St Mary's churchyard. However, there are many more...

There is an ancient legend which claims that at certain times of the year a long procession of ghostly coffins will slowly wind their way down Chapel Street towards St Mary's, this is an omen of doom, best avoided. This incredible spectacle does, surprisingly, have a basis in historical fact. Chapel street (previously 'Our Lady Street') used to be on the main route of funeral processions in the town and was nicknamed a 'death road' or 'corpse way'.

The 18th century Georgian House Hotel also claims it's own resident ghost, seen by many and there are a couple of other 'accommodation providers' who claim ghostly inhabitants.

One evening, a few years ago, two police officers were driving down Chapel Street when they suddenly saw an old lady sitting on a rocking chair in the window of an antique shop, slowly rocking. The driver stopped and reversed back up the street, only to find that she had gone. On further investigation, it seemed there was no such person in the property and nobody had an explanation for her appearance.

Coincidentally, the vicarage of St Mary's is also said to be haunted by an old lady in a rocking chair. This figure has frequently been seen in an upstairs living room of this early 18th century building and is believed to be a kindly soul.

The Acorn Theatre, near Chapel Street, claims to have the ghost of an actor who died on stage. Many people feel very unnerved, while others claim to have seen a figure.

Pubs in Chapel Street also live up to their reputation for frequently being haunted. The Turks Head is another of the places to lay claim to the ghost of Mrs Baines, with many strange things happening. The Abbey Restaurant, formerly the Zero was believed to also be haunted by an old lady with a pastime for moving things. The Dolphin Tavern has several well known ghosts and the Globe was built on the site of a former haunted building. Also the Regent Hotel and Restaurant is said to be haunted by a lady ghost seen by numerous people in the restaurant and upstairs area. People have also heard mysterious footsteps and found sand behind locked doors. She is believed to be a former servant of this 400 year old building.

There are many other ghostly tales and haunted properties but one of the most interesting centres on 62 Chapel Street.

This is the 'Arcade' and is a building which was built in the early nineteenth century for a sea captain. Originally there was a kitchen downstairs, said to be controlled by an irascible cook, who hated interference in her domain. This area is currently a small unit, available to let, however, it is frequently empty as nobody seems willing to lease it for long. Many people have heard banging and crashing noises coming from the shop, "when it is empty", and almost everybody senses a 'bad tempered' presence. Indeed, many believe that the cook's ghost is still haunting the shop, desperately annoyed to find her kitchen gone. The current owner of the shop directly above, regularly hears strange noises and will rarely visit his shop after dark for fear of the 'ghost'. Also it seems that at times of disruption in the building, the noises become more intense.

Can the bad tempered cook still be in her beloved kitchen, trying to scare her unwanted intruders?

HUMPHRY DAVY'S GHOST?

There is a building in Market Jew Street, Penzance which is well known for being the site where Sir Humphry Davy was born. It lies just a stones throw from the statue of Penzance's most famous son and is currently a shoe shop and restaurant. It is also yet another place which is prey to apparently supernatural goings on.

Forty years ago the upstairs was a popular cafe. At the time a girl aged fifteen worked there and had some strange experiences. One day her boss went out, leaving the girl on her own in the cafe. After a while she suddenly heard a noise in the back and went out to see what was happening. She then spotted a pair of legs disappearing out of sight up the stairs. She was sure her boss had not returned and had not noticed anyone pass her so she quickly went upstairs herself. She got to the top of the stairs and was astonished to find that there was nobody there. They could not have passed her and she was positive that she had seen someone going up there. It was then that she suddenly realised that the legs she had seen were not altogether normal. She could picture them in her mind and realised that who ever it was had been wearing a pair of very old fashioned shoes, with buckles and they had also been wearing tights and an old fashioned ankle suspender. She was now both bemused and a little frightened. When her boss returned she told him about her story and he confirmed that it had not been him. Neither of them saw the legs again but they did experience other frequent events. For example, doors would often open by themselves and strange noises would be heard. Also items such as crockery would often be found rearranged over night, when no one had been in the building. The events became so regular that the staff started to joke about "the ghost" and soon nicknamed him "Davy" in reference to the history of the building. Is it possible that there was a ghost here? and if so is it feasible to even propose that it was that of Sir Humphry Davy? The truth is that with all such things it is impossible to confirm and the fact is that many other people throughout history have lived or worked here. It does though create speculation about what was occurring forty years ago. Furthermore, there have been other people over subsequent years who have felt very uneasy here, heard noises, or claimed that things have moved around. However, there have not been any such clear sightings and as yet nobody has spotted any signs of a miners lamp or chemistry set!

Market Jew Street

There are several other properties in Market Jew Street which claim to have a ghostly reputation. Firstly, there is a set of shops in the lower part of the street which were originally built over the sight of a chapel and a small cemetery. There are people who remember the exhumation and subsequent building work and some even claim to have seen several coffins being removed over forty years ago. Some of these buildings, it is claimed, have eerie atmospheres and in one in particular several members of staff have been unnerved by a terrible atmosphere upstairs, refusing to spend any time in the eerie rooms.

Also in Market Jew Street there is a restaurant situated above a popular newsagent. Many years ago this was a family house and it is believed that a spiteful old lady lived here. She would often look after children and would do horrible things to them (for example she would often wake them at night by pinching them). She eventually died and afterwards several people living in the house claimed to see the ghost of an old lady. The description perfectly matched the old sadist, a fact confirmed by her own daughter. It was also claimed that doors would open by themselves and all sorts of other strange and unexplainable things occurred. It is said that such episodes carried on after the property became a dentist and also when it was turned into a restaurant. I myself worked at the restaurant when I was sixteen and was often bemused by doors which would open, only for nobody to come in. I always presumed that a customer had changed their mind but now I have researched the history, I am not so sure!

GHOSTLY FOOTSTEPS

Amongst ghostly phenomenon, footsteps are experienced on a large scale. In all sorts of strange places: houses, castles, dark lanes, smugglers tunnels and many other places besides, people report hearing phantom steps, belonging to an unseen person. I have included here two distinctive examples from Penzance.

Daniel Place, Penzance

A couple of years ago I was talking to a man on holiday in the area. He was staying in a property in Daniel Place which surrounds a courtyard area. Years ago, where the small houses are now, there stood 'Queens Garage'. The man proceeded to tell me how he kept hearing footsteps walking across the courtyard but whenever he looked there was nothing there. The footsteps had disturbed him and he could not explain how they were occurring. He had looked there immediately and seen no one. I could not then and still cannot explain these footsteps. However, I received a letter from a man a few months later which I found intriguing. The man wrote how he had worked at Queens garage years before. He accurately described the thin, tall, granite walls, the huge doorways, cobbled floor and horse stalls for cars. Then he wrote how one evening he was working on a car. It was a cold, dark, winter evening but not late. Suddenly, he heard "a heavy, man's footsteps walk up the centre of the garage to the little office". He was then waiting to hear them return and for someone to speak but this did not happen. He came out from the car and walked to the office but to his astonishment there was nobody there. He was deeply unnerved and decided to finish up and leave work. The next day he related the story to his boss who proceeded to say "so you've heard it too then". There seemed no explanation but the two events seem to be almost certainly linked. Perhaps we may never know who is causing the mysterious footsteps.

Rosevean Road, Penzance

In 1845 a horrific murder was committed at a house in Rosevean Road, near the Catholic church. A man named "Ellison" had been lodging at the house and had killed the landlady, a woman named "Mrs Seaman". The murder coincided with a time of great celebration in the town as the new pier was being opened. Therefore, it caused great consternation amongst local people. Soon afterwards the house stood empty but of the people who have lived in the house since, many have described feeling an ominous presence and a feeling of despair and sadness emanating through the rooms of the house. In fact, several people have moved out of the house, over the years, citing such experiences as the main reason. Amazingly, if these emanations are supernatural then it seems they are not restricted to the house itself. Many people have regularly heard footsteps trudging down Rosevean Road itself. Particularly in the dead of night, numerous people have heard the unmistakable sound of a person walking in the centre of the street. People have often looked quickly out of their window to see who the person is, only to discover the street is empty. There seems to be no explanation. A few years ago a man was returning home just after midnight when he heard footsteps behind him. They were quite close so he quickly turned to see who was following him, expecting to see one of his neighbours. However, as he swung around he was surprised to see an empty street. He claims he can not have been mistaken and there was certainly no time for a person to have disappeared out of sight. Of course these footsteps could be caused by something other than the ghost of the murder victim. Nevertheless, it is certainly a remarkable coincidence that strange footsteps in the street happen to be heard in the vicinity of the house where the murder was committed. Can it be the ghost of Mrs Seaman? walking the road in despair; or as others have claimed perhaps the spirit of Ellison is walking here out of guilt, fated to endlessly walk the road where he claimed his victim.

THE BREAD STREET "GYPSY"

Bread Street in Penzance is one of the quietest, yet most haunted areas of Penzance. There are many tales including: a ghostly old woman seen walking up the Arcade Steps (see 'Ghost Hunting page.29); a Boer war soldier in a back lane; and phantom footsteps and cries from animals killed in the slaughter houses, which stood here in the last century. However, the story that fascinates me the most is one with several independent witnesses whose stories corroborate very closely.

Less than a year ago I heard a story relating to Bread street, which although fascinating at the time, I had no conclusive evidence for. I was told that a man had been driving down Bread Street between 5 and 6 a.m. one morning, on his way to work. In the car headlights he suddenly saw a figure walking across in front of his car. He quickly slowed down the car and saw that the figure was an elderly lady. He described her as being "gypsy like", as she was wearing a long flowing dress and a dark shawl. He was still waiting for her to cross when another car came in the opposite direction. This car also came to a halt, presumably because the driver had also seen the elderly lady and was allowing her to cross in safety. The first driver watched as she slowly made her way across the narrow street and then something incredible happened. To his utter astonishment the woman suddenly vanished before his very eyes. He could not believe what he had seen and thought he must be mistaken but he suddenly realised there was a way to check. So he quickly got out of his car and approached the other driver who was sat staring dumbfounded at the road. He asked if he had seen the elderly lady, which he and his passengers confirmed they had. Indeed they went on to speak of how they had slowed down for her and were shocked to see her simply disappear. "One second she was there, the next gone". There had been nowhere for her to go and no explanation for this remarkable event, nevertheless several witnesses had clearly seen an elderly lady simply vanish.

(This is a spot where I have seen dogs acting very strangely and electrical equipment often fails). It certainly was an incredible tale and one which I planned to investigate at a later date. I spend a lot of time in Bread Street on my ghost tours and so vowed to research further. Then one evening I was with a group of people in Bread Street when a gentleman came up and told us about a strange experience he himself had had there. One day he was walking here on his own when he suddenly saw an elderly lady wearing a long black dress with a very pale face, walking in the middle of the street. Something about her made him feel uneasy. As she walked past he felt very cold and turned to look at her, only to be surprised to find there was no sign. It was as if she had vanished. He was absolutely convinced he had seen a ghost and was at pains to convince me and the group that his story was absolutely genuine. The two stories were strikingly similar and both were describing the same location (the lower end of Bread Street). I was now deeply interested to find out more. Over the subsequent months I have now spoken to several other people who have had identical experiences. All of them have described an elderly lady, wearing a long dress, a shawl and "Bohemian" clothing. They also all describe seeing her suddenly disappear without explanation.

Furthermore, I also believe I may have traced the most likely candidate for the identity of the ghost. It seems that an elderly lady had owned an antiques shop in the Arcade Steps years ago. She had loved the shop but during old age she had become very eccentric and confused and gone to live elsewhere in the town. She wished to return to live at the shop and became very upset that she could not and soon afterwards she died in hospital. Many people have talked about the lady and said how she used to wear "eccentric" clothing, long dresses, shawls, long coats and so on and one of her friends informed me of a piece of information which is extremely poignant . She told me that her friend, whose name I will keep confidential purely out of respect, had "gypsy blood in her". This one piece of information always reminds me of the first description I received of the figure..."Gypsy Like".

THE OLD ONES, MOUSEHOLE

Through many generations in the fishing village of Mousehole people have talked about the many ghosts who reside around the village. Many of the old fishing houses and harbour cottages are said to accommodate their own supernatural resident. The 'Old Ones', as they have often been named, it seems are everywhere. In my last book I spoke about the old man who seemed to still be enjoying "his pipe, his cottage and his favourite place", years after his death. By no means however, is he the only supernatural visitor to Mousehole. For example the former Kiegwin mansion is believed to be haunted by several former members of the Kiegwin family. There is a guest house whose visitor's book is full with guests comments about the "friendly ghost". The Ship Inn is believed to be haunted by a strange man in the upper corridor and nearby in a lane, people have been known to hear footsteps belonging to a large group of people coming towards them, heading towards the harbour. However, as the footsteps get closer it soon becomes apparent that they belong to no visible people. However, this does not stop dogs acting as if they can see something, cowering, growling or barking. Many people believe these to be the ghosts of fishermen from long ago. There are many more besides but perhaps one of the most interesting stories (and dare I say credible) is the following, awe inspiring tale.

South View Terrace

After an appeal for information in a local newspaper I visited a likeable lady who had lived in a house in South View Terrace, Mousehole about fifteen years previously. She and her family had experienced some very strange experiences in the house which she began to recount to me, nervously, in as much detail as possible. I heard about her terrifying encounters and saw her grow more and more agitated as she remembered. I soon realised I had heard an almost identical tale before about a house in the same area of Mousehole and the similarities soon led me to believe that the separate people had almost certainly lived in the same house at different times, yet experienced the same peculiar phenomena. Ultimately these people had all been forced to leave the house and as you read the story you may well understand why.

The house is approximately two hundred years old and is believed to have been built by a man who later lived in the house. In the 1980s a family, I will call Bartram, bought the house and moved in. Very soon after, the Bartrams all felt a strange "presence", a feeling of coldness and an indescribable smell, terrible, "like sewerage". This smell would appear very suddenly in the lounge area, stay for about ten minutes and abruptly disappear again. Several people smelt this but nobody could come up with an explanation. There were no drains, leaks or nearby toilets. At other times a much more pleasant smell would also appear, a perfumed smell as of cut flowers. This also appeared only for brief periods of time and was also unexplainable. One day Mrs Bartram was sitting in the lounge with her friend, fawning over her baby son. Suddenly the two ladies both clearly saw the push chair shoot across the room as if being pushed, again there was no explanation. The two women were concerned enough to inform Mr Bartram who was downstairs. It was then that he told them, that for a while he had noticed things moving around. For example his tools would often go missing only to turn up later in an unlikely place. Soon after this, furniture started to move in the house, seemingly by itself and other smaller objects would often be moved while nobody was in the room. One day Mr and Mrs Bartram were decorating in a downstairs room. They had put a coat of varnish on the floor only to realise they had been remiss in starting at the wrong end from the light switch. This meant they had to leave the light on when they retired to bed. The next morning they were staggered to find that the light had been turned off by itself, yet there were no footprints on the floor.

About the time of these events they were told by their neighbour that their two houses were haunted. She had apparently seen a figure on several occasions and it was said that the two (semi-detached) properties were visited by the same ghost. She believed him to be the ghost of the man who had built the houses. She had no more information about him except that he seemed to have an irrational hatred of smoking. The Bartrams were not sure about this latest news but Mr Bartram in particular preferred to look for more rational explanations.

Soon after Mrs Bartram entered a bedroom to find puddles of water everywhere. There seemed to be no reason, there was no leaky roof, no supply of water in the bedroom and it was a dry day outside. Then her husband was taking a shower in the bathroom. He stepped on to the bathroom floor and suddenly felt what seemed to be a hand on his shoulder. He instinctively swung around and put his own hand up to his shoulder. There was nobody there but he discovered a strange white powder on his hand and shoulder. How did it get there? He had just showered and had no explanation.

By now the family slept with all the lights on in the house and moved their baby son into their bedroom, out of fear.

At Christmas Mrs Bartram was in her lounge decorating the tree, by hanging up Christmas baubles. She took a break and suddenly she saw out of the corner of her eye a bauble come flying towards her. She cried out and immediately the object stopped and fell to the floor inches from her face. Surprisingly it was not damaged, however her nerves were. There had been nobody else in the room apart from her baby asleep in his push chair and he was clearly not responsible.

A few weeks later the Bartrams were in their front room with their baby son and Mr Bartram's daughter, nobody else was in the house. The baby needed a change so Mrs Bartram went upstairs to fetch the necessary items from the bedroom. She then returned via the only flight of stairs to the lounge. Everybody else was still in the lounge and she suddenly realised she had forgotten something and returned up the stairs to the bedroom. As she walked in to the room she got the shock of her life. A thick, heavy mirror had been moved across the room and was now lying up against a chest of drawers. It had been hanging on the wall and was now on the floor on the opposite side of the room. It was a square mirror, so could not possibly have rolled. Besides, the mirror had been hung over a dressing table covered in all sorts of cans, bottles and cosmetics. If the mirror had fallen it would certainly have knocked these flying but they were still very much in place. What was particularly disturbing were a set of scratch marks discovered on the wall behind where the picture had been.

Overall, the family lived in the house for about eighteen months. Many other peculiar and startling things occurred and by the end their nerves had been thoroughly frayed. Often a dark, ominous sense of despair and depression filled the house and people often sensed a disturbing presence. They felt that a "black cloud was constantly hanging over" them and everything seemed to go wrong. If, as seems likely, the house was indeed haunted what could be the explanation?

The man who built the adjoining houses, about two hundred years ago, had lived in the Bartram's house and it is believed he was very fond of the place. Furthermore, it is told that he died in the house, in fact it is believed that he died in what is now the bathroom, the scene of several strange events. Could this man, this former resident , have still possibly been residing in the house after all those years, after his own death? If so, then he may well have remained there after the Bartrams departure. There is some strong evidence to suggest that other subsequent residents have experienced great fear, distress and foreboding and other more tangible experiences including many almost identical to those encountered by the Bartram family. It is difficult to dismiss the Bartram story, they certainly cannot be accused of making it up or being victims of over imagination. Can it be then that this is just another example of Mousehole's famous "Old Ones", a ghost from the past, unable to leave the alluring village, now so popular with tourists?

MYSTERIOUS MONKS

Ghosts belonging to Monks are very common indeed, so not surprisingly, there are also several examples of them in Cornwall. Here are two tales relating to the area of Newlyn.

Gwavas

At the top of Newlyn (near Penzance) is the area of Gwavas. This now mostly consists of a modern housing estate. However, parts of it are quite old, indeed one particular street is approximately two hundred years old and was built on top of much older properties. Many of these houses look over a set of fields towards a farm house. It is rumoured that this area was at one stage monastery land and so would have been frequented by Benedictine monks. In modern times several people have described seeing a strange hooded figure in a brown cloak from their window. They have often gone outside to find there is nobody there.

On one occasion three people in a house clearly saw a person of this description walk past their window as if heading to the front door. They were so certain of this, that one of them got up and went to the door in anticipation of him knocking. They opened the door and found the doorstep empty. The path leading to the door is flanked by a wall and so the only exit is via the path past the window. Yet nobody inside had seen the 'man' return. It was as if he had vanished.

Paul

Near Newlyn is the village of Paul and here on the road from Paul to St Buryan the ghosts of hooded monks have also been seen. They may be linked to the land at Gwavas or the Benedictine monastery on nearby St Michael's mount centuries ago.

THE FISHERMEN GHOSTS

There are hundreds of stories about the ghosts of fishermen and sailors, around the many ports and harbours throughout Cornwall. Tales of death and intrigue, terror and adventure. It is often difficult with some of these tales to identify the difference between fact and legend, myth and reality. However, here are a couple of tales which are certainly genuine.

Newlyn

In West Penwith, adjoining Penzance, is the famous fishing village of Newlyn. There are many old fisherman's cottages with tales to tell. However, one cottage in particular has a story which is especially compelling. I was recently told the story by a lady who lived in the cottage a couple of years ago and one evening her and her partner had a very unnerving encounter.

That evening they were sat in their front room watching television when they heard a noise. Looking up they were shocked to see a strange man standing inside their cottage, by the front door. They had no idea how he had arrived there or what he was doing. The lady's partner leapt to his feet to challenge the intruder, described as a "big, burly, fisherman type". When the intruder did not speak he sped across the room and charged at him. To his astonishment he suddenly found himself sprawled on the floor. He had seemingly gone straight through the man who had erstwhile appeared perfectly solid and human. The 'fisherman' then walked across the room towards the bedroom and walked straight through the wall. At this point the couple were even more disturbed, because their baby was asleep in that bedroom. The lady ran into the room and snatched up her baby son before noticing that there was no sign of the man but the room was uncharacteristically cold. The couple were by now petrified and believed they had been the victim of a ghostly encounter. They went back into the front room and sat there for several hours, terrified and unable to sleep. The house remained absolutely freezing until sometime that night they heard a noise again. To their horror they again saw the burly fisherman, this time leaving the bedroom and heading for the front door. He then proceeded to walk straight through the door. They ran and checked outside but there was no sign of him. Immediately the house warmed up again and the couple felt calmer. However, their experiences were enough to convince them to leave the property as soon as possible.

In itself it sounds like a remarkable event and there seems no reason to disbelieve the lady who told me the story. Nevertheless one witness is never sufficient, so I set out to conduct my own research. I discovered that a subsequent resident had experienced an identical episode and a former resident had also sensed a presence late at night. But perhaps most remarkably I discovered that only a few years before a previous resident had been a fisherman, a man who had lived in the cottage for many years before dying there. He had often returned home late in the evening before setting off early in the morning to go out to sea. A coincidence? Judge for yourself.

Hayle

I have also been told a story, in many ways similar, about a house near Hayle harbour. A man living there would often detect a strong smell of fish late in the evening, sometimes accompanied by the smell of pipe smoke. He tried in vain to discover the source but there seemed to be no explanation. However, he soon discovered that the smell always occurred at about 9.00p.m. He made some more enquiries around the area but no one had an explanation. Then by chance he discovered that a former resident of the house had been a fisherman and by a strange coincidence he had always come home at about 9.00p.m. The man was now deceased but it is just possible he was still returning to his former house, after a hard days work, to relax and enjoy his pipe!

BODRIGGY HOUSE, HAYLE

The current Bodriggy House in Hayle was rebuilt around 1718 and is now split into two homes. However, the property is much older than this and was originally one large building. As with many similar properties there is a great deal of history surrounding it, much of which is unclear. Nevertheless, a strongly forged disagreement between two sisters, hundreds of years ago, may well have resulted in some strange and perhaps supernatural occurrences in the recent past.

I was sent the main components of the following story by a lady who worked at Bodriggy approximately ten years ago. I have little reason to doubt her claims to have experienced, along with others, some strange and unexplainable occurrences at the house.

Linda often worked alone in the house, while the owners were away on business. She was able to come and go as she pleased. However, she always felt uneasy when alone in the house, without knowing why. She would frequently get a feeling that she was being watched, although she was completely alone. As the dark winter evenings approached Linda found herself avoiding the house and would often take along somebody for company, rather than visit alone. Sometimes she would take her youngest daughter along with her, but never felt comfortable leaving her on her own. One day her eldest daughter accompanied her to Bodriggy. They had only been there a short time when suddenly her daughter came running up the stairs. She had apparently kept hearing noises in the dining room. Thinking it was her mother she had called out to her, without reply. She had then entered the dining room, only to find no sign of anybody. She did, however, observe some keys, mysteriously swinging in the lock. They both investigated immediately but found no one, but the room had become icy cold. They were so anxious they immediately left the house.

Another day Linda's mother accompanied her to the house. She had not been informed of any of Linda's recent experiences, nevertheless, she immediately remarked on the unnaturally cold temperature in certain rooms and was extremely relieved when they finally left, feeling that "something was just not right".

Then one afternoon Linda was working in the lounge when the room suddenly became very cold again, she shivered. She became convinced that there was somebody else in the room and swung around. There she caught sight of a strange 'mist', passing the open door. She shivered again, uncontrollably and immediately fled towards the door to close it, she was terrified. Then, at that moment, she heard a car pulling up outside and was utterly relieved to see the owner approaching the house.

It seemed that Linda's appearance was so strange, "pale as a sheet and shaking", that the owner became immediately concerned and asked her what was wrong. After telling her about her experiences, Linda learnt some new, disturbing information. Many years before, two sisters had lived in the house and quarrelled bitterly. Ultimately their disagreement led to them dividing the house into two and forbidding entry to the other to their own side. Incredibly, it seemed that the dividing wall had been situated in the places where the coldness now appeared. The owner herself and several other visitors had also apparently seen a figure standing here. It was believed that the ghost of one of the sisters was continuing to haunt the house and had frequently been seen materialising through the wall, the place she had been forbidden to cross during her lifetime.

Linda was still terrified and decided to seek help from a psychic friend. She was then instructed to attempt to "lift" the unhappy emotions in the house. Thus she returned alone and nervously spoke out the necessary words she had learned, several times. She walked through the house and completed the task.

Incredibly from that day onwards, it seems a change came over Bodriggy House. The house became a much happier place and no more sightings of the strange figure, seen for many years before, were now reported. It was as if the unhappy spirit had been moved on, perhaps thanks to Linda's help.

SKIDDEN HILL, ST IVES

St Ives has, and always has had, a lot of ghosts. Indeed, it continued to employ a professional ghost layer in the mid nineteenth century, long after most towns had stopped employing such questionable characters, such was the reputation of the town. There are stories of ghostly horses; Victorian figures; strange ghostly men; eerie presences; poltergeists; the famous lady of the lamp; phantom ships and sailors; mysterious footsteps; smugglers and most of the other well known types of ghosts.

On Skidden Hill, however, you may encounter one or more ghosts, of a dubious reputation.

In the mid nineteenth century a common 'doss house' was situated on Skidden Hill. All sorts of travellers, beggars, tramps, vagrants and drunks frequented the building and surrounding area. The house was known as "Beggars Roost", and most local people, unsurprisingly, avoided Skidden Hill at all costs. People who did walk here would often find themselves confronted by several 'wretched' characters, pleading with them for alms. It would be unwise to refuse as often such people were assaulted, either verbally or physically. After many years the house was closed and is no more, although for a long time St Ives' unwanted continued to linger around Skidden Hill.

Today, nothing of that sad past remains, Skidden Hill is a safe and respectable place, except that some people suggest it is unable to completely throw off it's unsavoury past. There are suggestions that one or more of it's former patrons, those of ill repute, still hang around the street, well over a century after their deaths.

In the 1980s a young German man was staying in the area and decided to go for an early morning stroll (around 6.00a.m.). He was walking down the hill when he spotted a dishevelled looking figure crouched by the side of the road. There was no sign of movement, so he became quite concerned. He walked over to within a few feet and suddenly felt very cold, even though it was a warm summer's morning. Furthermore, he had

26

an indescribable feeling that he should not touch the man. He quickly ran to his accommodation nearby and sought help. Soon he returned with his wife and another man, only to find to his astonishment that the figure had gone, though it had been less than five minutes. He described him as wearing "very worn and old fashioned clothes", and being "very scruffy and unshaved".

A few years later another man was walking up the hill, one late evening (about 10.00pm) when he spotted a man standing by the side of the road with his hand outstretched. He also had a hat lying on the floor, so he presumed he must be a beggar. He was surprised to see someone here at such a late hour but decided to avoid a confrontation and reached into his pocket for some loose change, throwing them into the hat. The beggar did not utter a sound, so the man quickly walked away up the hill. However, after a few paces he could not resist glancing back. To his utter astonishment the man was no longer there, he had simply vanished. He walked back to the spot where the man had been and was amazed to find his coins lying on the floor and the hat also gone. He was positive that the beggar could not possibly have removed the coins and left in such a short space of time.

There have also been numerous other sightings of other dark, mysterious figures; men with torn and dated clothing, accompanied by a cold and terrifying sense of being around something "not altogether of this world".

The mystery continues as to who these strange figures are, but one explanation may be that they are the ghosts of the forsaken men who frequented Skidden Hill in the Nineteenth century, still remaining, to this day, in their former "haunt"!

There is also said to be an old house in the middle of Skidden Hill which is haunted. At one stage the building was owned by a local doctor and it is he who is still said to reside in the house, uninvited.

MYSTERIOUS LANDS END

Lands End is perhaps the most famous location in Cornwall. Nothing lies beyond it's cliffs bar the Isles of Scilly and hundreds of miles of deep, rolling Atlantic Ocean. However, if you accept local legend this may not altogether be true. For there are many who claim that the lost Lands of Lyonesse lie under it's unforgiving waters. Witnesses claim to have heard ghostly church bells sounding from out at sea and fisherman will swear they have seen steeples and towers underneath the water.

Lands End itself also has it's share of ghostly activity. A few years ago, strange happenings were observed by two reliable witnesses in a building at Lands End. On numerous occasions they would enter the building in the morning to find the strange sight of 'Sea Pinks', scattered over the floor. These flowers were often stuck in the carpet as if trodden down. There was no explanation, the building was locked and unoccupied over night, yet the flowers reoccurred time after time. Also, it was sometimes felt that they were "not alone" and dust would appear in places already cleaned. It is interesting to note that many years ago the building was used to lay out dead bodies (it still has a coffin hatch). Perhaps some unseen person was returning to the building to place flowers, as would have been done many years before. But who, could enter a locked building?

Also at Lands End is the Lands End Hotel. This has also been prone to supernatural goings on, confirmed by several witnesses. During the war, American soldiers stayed here and their presence seems not altogether to have diminished. Also there is a particular room where several years ago, supernatural activities were reported on an almost daily basis. Chamber maids would often open the curtains and lock the room, yet when they returned later they would find the curtains closed again. Objects were known to move and disappear and several people felt a presence in the room. After years of anxious staff and guests, the hotel decided to change the room by adding a wall. However, activities seemed to continue nevertheless.

On the road between Lands End and St Ives several independent people have reported driving on the road and suddenly having the feeling that they are being chased. The overwhelming opinion is that there are horses and their riders galloping after them. This is an area where revenue officers would have often chased smugglers in the nineteenth century.

Castle Carn Brea

Near Lands End is 'Castle Carn Brea'. This is an area popular with campers, though not always for long! Several visitors have heard an unnerving sound of horses galloping towards them. It is believed that the area is haunted by a group of horsemen riding down the hill. One summer, a lady I spoke to was staying in a camping van in the car park when her and her husband heard a peculiar noise. They described it as being similar to the noise the 'Wall of Death' motorbikes used to make. They went outside and although it was a lovely clear moonlit night they could see nothing which would explain the sound. Many years later, they came across the story about the ghostly horsemen by chance and were then sure they had heard them too.

Porthcurno

Porthcurno is famous for it's beaches and the nearby Minack Theatre but it is also quite well known for another story. Many centuries ago, Porthcurno is said to have been a place where many ships came to land, before it became a beach. It is said that phantom tall ships have been spotted off the coast nearby, sailing up and down. These are believed to be portents before a disaster, warning of rough storms and lost ships. The number of ships seen is said to predict the number of ships which will go down in the storm. When fog is rolling in a ghostly black rigger has been reported coming in from the sea and gliding up over the sands, across dry land, where the former harbour would have been.

Between Porthcurno and Nanjisal Cove the infamous Demon Tregeagle is rumoured to make his presence known. Some believe that this evil magistrate was sent here as punishment to commit the endless task of sweeping the sands between the two. His howls are said to be heard around the cliffs at particularly stormy times. Also around this rugged cliff line the famous sight of "Jack Harry's Lanterns" is often seen. These are a set of phantom lights, prevalent in West Cornwall. Rayon gas? Ball lightning? or spectral lights, once the spirits of lost seamen? I'll let you decide!

There is also said to be the ghost of Ben Smith (or other alias) walking across the cliff paths in the area. This spectral being, possibly a smuggler, has been described as wearing very old fashioned clothes and a tri-corne hat and to be carrying a barrel, which may be difficult as many people claim he has no visible limbs.

Sennen

At a Sennen hotel, a little girl was once killed by a stage coach. She was knocked down and killed instantly in a terribly sad event. Ever since her ghost is believed to haunt the hotel itself. Many people staying or working in room 6 have described hearing a child's voice asking them to play with her. She is never seen but is often heard. Why people are so sure it is the girl who died is not clear but I suspect that not too many other young children were killed here.

Many years ago an Irish ship was wrecked off Sennen. The only survivor was a young lady who swam to shore. There she clung to a rock hoping for rescue, unable to climb the dangerous rocks to safety. Many days later her body was discovered, it seems she died of a mixture of thirst, exhaustion and exposure. It is claimed that on stormy nights people have seen a figure of a young lady clinging to the rock now known as "The Irish Lady".

THE MINERS

Carnyorth lies very close to the larger villages of St Just and Pendeen. It is an area deeply associated with tin mining and close to Geevor and Levant mines. Therefore many people living there years ago would have worked in the mine. In 1919 there was a disaster at Levant mine when an engine rod snapped and thirty one workers were killed. It was a tragedy which stayed in peoples memories for years to come and some other distressing memory of the tragedy seems to linger on to this day. Several people have been walking on the Cornish coast when they have suddenly felt very cold, shivers go down their spine and they suddenly feel a deep sense of despair. It is usually later that they find out that the place where they were walking is actually directly over the exact location of the terrible accident, a place where survivors and bodies remained for days before they could be rescued. We can only imagine what sort of despair would of been suffered by these people. Does something of it linger on?

It is also said that one of the victims of the disaster at Levant may haunt a site at Carnyorth. A figure has been seen crossing the court yard of the old school buildings and entering what is now the toilet block. On investigation nobody is then found in this building. Many people have seen this white figure (including my own brother) and it is believed to be the ghost of a child killed in the mining disaster who went to the school.

I have also heard of another very interesting ghostly tale about Carnyorth. About five years ago a bus was driving through Carnyorth with the driver and one female passenger. As they were coming along Cresswell's Road (leading to Botallack) a woman wearing a long riding coat suddenly stepped out in front of the bus. The driver slammed his foot on the brake but could not stop in time. He was horrified as the bus went straight through the figure, which then disappeared. There was certainly no longer anybody there but they had both seen her clearly. Indeed the female passenger was so distraught the driver had to leave the bus and fetch her husband to come and comfort her.

TRURO GHOSTS

Like any city Truro has it's fair share of ghosts. From Poltergeists (see 'Ghost Hunting...') and rattling chains (Comprigney field) and that favourite of spectral visitors the monk's ghost (at the William the 4th public house) to the common ghost of the murder victim (at The Star, Castle street) Truro seems to have them all and all those other well known ghostly types across the phantom scale. However, there are also some less 'classic' examples of hauntings in this the capital of Cornwall.

Lemon Street

In the Eighteenth, century Truro was a very fashionable place and Lemon Street contained many of it's elegant houses, of which many survive today. In one such house lies a series of offices. The basement of this building is used as a strong room. However, over the years many people working in the building have refused to enter the strong room alone at night. This is because many have experienced a feeling of "not being alone", an evil presence lurking behind the door. Numerous people have independently reported this feeling, while others have also claimed to have heard strange noises coming from this empty room. What is intriguing is the fact that in Edwardian times it is said that a man had hung himself in the cellars of the building (now the strong room). Many people believe it is his ghost now haunting the basement.

Boscawen Street

Some years ago an old scout master lived above a chemist shop in Boscawen street. He was often troubled by strange noises and what seems to be evidence of a resident ghost.

Several reliable witnesses heard the same noises. The stairs would creak, followed by a door slamming and a piano would suddenly start playing in an empty room. After a while the piano playing would cease, the door would slam once again and once more creaking footsteps would be heard on the stairs. Several people would claim that they thus felt a presence enter the room followed by the feeling that they were being watched or stared at. This proved to be quite unnerving and some people even described the feeling as being "evil". People were often known to look in the direction of this 'presence' but never saw anyone. Furthermore the upstairs room was investigated on several occasions while the piano playing was going on but there was never anybody there.

Some people had already had prior knowledge of the story before visiting the property, so their evidence is doubtful. However, several witnesses had no idea of the previous events and therefore no expectations, but nevertheless clearly reported the same noises. The owner subsequently did some research of the property and to his astonishment he found out that a former resident who had died in the house had been, of all things, a musician. Therefore if he was the ghost, his attraction to the piano is obvious.

Comprigney

On the North West outskirts of Truro lies the fields of Comprigney. It is believed that here was positioned a Gibbet, centuries before (in fact Comprigney is believed to translate as 'Field of the Gibbet') . Therefore we can presume that several unfortunate victims were hung and displayed to passers by. Can it be that this gruesome history can be related to the eerie sounds of rattling chains that have been heard here and are the shadowy figures in any way connected to the men whose corpses swung here as a testament to their alleged crimes?

BODMIN MOOR

There are so many tales around wild and desolate Bodmin Moor that they could fill several volumes on their own. Therefore I have selected a few of the more acceptable stories.

A few years ago a man was walking on Bodmin Moor when he suddenly became aware of a man on horseback riding towards him. The man came close enough for him to get a full view and he described him as wearing very old fashioned clothes with black and white embroidery, leather boots and a very large, wide brimmed hat. Suddenly the horseman stopped the horse and jumped down by the side. Immediately he started to fade and then both the man and the horse simply vanished. He was stunned and quickly returned to his car. He was convinced he had seen the ghost of a smuggler, perhaps fuelled by his earlier visit to Jamaica Inn. However, he did some research into old fashion and soon became convinced that he had seen a member of the nobility. The clothes struck him as being expensive but clearly from a bygone age, most likely the eighteenth century. What he was doing there is unclear but the man was convinced he was not of this world.

A very similar story comes from another location on Bodmin Moor. Some people suddenly became very cold and in the distance saw a horse approaching. It was running quite fast, getting progressively closer. When it came into full view they realised that it was rider less but incredibly was running several inches off the ground. It seemed to be floating in mid air and before they knew it suddenly vanished.

Another figure hovering off the ground has also been seen on Bodmin Moor. In an isolated place people have claimed to see a man walking across a sheer drop before arriving at the other side and disappearing.

A terrifying figure has also been spotted hanging from a tree. The man with a white shirt, black trousers and red neckerchief has remained in view long enough to deeply distress its witnesses before disappearing, just as quickly. Also the ghost of Charlotte Dymond is believed to walk over the moors since she was murdered in 1844 at Rough Tor and there are also stories about Dozemary Pool and the ghost of the Demon Tregeagle and the lady of the lake who claimed Excalibur.

At the village of Warleggan, in the South of the moor the ghost of the former vicar the Reverend Demsham has been seen by many at the former rectory. He is seen walking in the garden of his former home to and fro, in a dark coat and black hat. While alive he became a recluse who shunned his parishioners. He would often be seen alone wandering in the garden in deep thought, hands behind his back. Eventually he was found dead on his stairs with the house in a terrible state.

Finally, any description of ghosts on Bodmin Moor has to include the infamous Jamaica Inn at Bolventor. There are indeed several ghostly inhabitants who have been seen or heard on numerous occasions leading to an extremely ghostly reputation. Firstly, footsteps have been heard walking along an upstairs corridor and into a bedroom late at night. This is the same bedroom where people have claimed to have seen a figure standing by the door wearing a tri-corne hat and long overcoat. He is said to then walk past the bed and disappear through the wardrobe leaving the room icy cold. This may or may not be the same ghost that has been seen downstairs as well. A figure in a cloak and three cornered hat has also been spotted in the Du Maurier restaurant walking through a thick panelled door and a cloaked man has been viewed in the kitchen of the stable block on numerous occasions. Also a man in a tri-corne hat has been watched in the courtyard heading towards the Inn and vanishing. The stable block has also been the scene of other strange sounds. It is believed that the ghosts of smugglers are often heard here, either shouting or talking with a very strong Cornish dialect. In the past many members of staff have reported hearing strange conversations in what appears to be the native Cornish language (no longer spoken). Perhaps the most common sound to be heard at Jamaica Inn are those of horses footsteps and the rattle of a coaches wheels when no sign of either is present. These are either galloping or moving along the cobbles and on a few occasions the sound of heavy objects being unloaded has also been heard. Another ghostly figure on horseback has been seen on a few occasions. This man is usually seen on misty nights outside the Inn, apparently waiting for some unseen person. On the 2nd of August 2000 a man took a photograph of his wife and daughter inside the Inn and when the film was developed an unmistakable figure appeared behind them. The figure resembles a person but is quite distorted, dare I say "ghostlike". They have no explanation as there was seemingly nobody there when the photo was taken. Finally Jamaica Inn has one more ghostly visitor. A man is occasionally seen sitting mysteriously on a wall outside the Inn. He is believed to be the ghost of a man (possibly a sailor or smuggler) murdered some years ago. The unfortunate man was in the Inn when he was called outside. The next morning his body was found on Bodmin Moor, without explanation, and the culprit was never found. However, the man spotted outside the pub is believed to bear a striking resemblance to the murder victim. It has also been claimed that footsteps are sometimes heard in the bar just after one of his appearances and it is believed that the man is returning to finish the ale he left unfinished on the bar that fateful night.

Generally it is difficult to know how genuine the Jamaica Inn ghosts are. Many people visit after reading Daphne Du Maurier's book, half expecting to view smugglers ride up over the bleak moor and are victims of their own imagination. Nevertheless, many of the stories are well corroborated and appear surprisingly credible. Jamaica Inn has an amazing history, the truth of which we can only begin to imagine, so it is not difficult to assume that such a place should have it's ghosts.

LANHYDROCK HOUSE, BODMIN

Lanhydrock House near Bodmin is a much visited National Trust property set in beautiful gardens. The house was originally built in the seventeenth century on a site which was part of St Petroc's priory. Unfortunately most of the original building perished in a fire at the end of the nineteenth century. However, some very old parts do still remain. It is an historic property and so may be expected to have one or more ghosts in residence. Paul Holden, House Manager tells me that "there is no evidence of ghosts being in residence here at the house". Others though are not so sure! Several members of the conservation staff have all claimed to have seen a man walking the house in a top hat wearing Victorian clothing. Perhaps this is linked to the fire. I mentioned previously, or he may simply be a former resident of the house, still wandering his former home. Over the years many people have also claimed to see the famous "Grey Lady". A solid ghostly figure dressed in dark grey has been seen walking down the first floor corridor and the Gallery and sometimes in the Great Room, which pre- dates the fire, either standing or sitting in a chair, before slowly fading away. There is also said by some to be a very strange presence in one of the bedrooms, certainly female but of no visual appearance. Another story suggests that in the 17th century, at the time of the English Civil War, a man was accused of robbing the house and sentenced to death by the Royalist Army. The unfortunate fellow was then taken to the Gatehouse and swiftly hung. It is claimed that a figure, presumed to be his ghost, has been seen outside the Gatehouse at night.

It is not evident how often these ghosts have been seen in recent times but another reoccurring phenomenon has been experienced recently. On the Ground Floor is the aptly named "Smoking Room". Nowadays smoking is strictly forbidden. Nevertheless, on many occasions members of staff have opened the room and smelt a distinctive smell of fresh cigar smoke.

The identity of the majority of Lanhydrock's ghosts is unclear but over the years staff and visitors alike have encountered them. The reader may well wish to visit to see for themselves or perhaps they may agree with Paul Holden "Living in the property I can say with some conviction that I have not and, needless to say, do not wish to meet any of these occurrences".

BODMIN GAOL

Just outside Bodmin centre lies the depressing Bodmin Gaol. For many years this was used to house all sorts of criminals and law breakers. It was a dank, rat infested, wretched place full of despair and misery. Many people knew this to be their last place on earth, either dying in their cell from disease or quickly despatched by the executioner after sentence of death. What if anything remains of this testament to a time less forgiving than our own? Any visitor to the gaol can quickly imagine it's former condition and picture the suffering from within it's walls but it may be that something more tangible has remained at the site. Many people have heard the sound of rattling keys coming from across the prison, yet there is nobody around to make such a noise. Others have heard the eerie sound of footsteps approaching across the floor, only for nobody to materialise. Hushed voices have also been heard and more disturbingly some people have seen a fleeting form move quickly, just in the periphery of their vision before it quickly vanishes. Overwhelmingly, people sense an unmistakable feeling of depression, a desperate all encompassing misery surrounding them. Can this all just be the imagination of susceptible people, unnerved by their whereabouts or can it be that something more substantial has remained from a time long passed?

THE LOST GARDENS OF HELIGAN

Between St Austell and Mevagissey lies the staggering Lost Gardens of Heligan. These abandoned gardens have been rediscovered and rebuilt over the last few years and have a sinister, haunted, reputation. Many members of staff, for instance, will not venture into certain garden areas.

Firstly, there is the 'Lost Valley' an area where people sense a peculiar silence, described as an "eerie, deathly hush". Others have sensed a feeling of overwhelming sadness. It is a place where people have claimed to see dark shadows moving around, floating and drifting, before disappearing. It is also a place where dogs have acted very strangely.

In the 'Crystal Grotto', an area where people have sensed a peculiar presence. A man once described seeing a figure walk across the ground before walking into a wall and vanishing. The 'Melon Garden is another place where strange things have occurred. People have claimed to see things move. For instance people have seen plant pots lift by themselves. Others have described feeling an acute sense of 'no longer being alone'. It is believed that the area is haunted by a former gardener, long dead, who loves the place so much he will not leave.

In the old 'Heligan Woods", there is a warning that people can become disorientated. This is because so many have sensed an uneasy feeling of losing their way and feeling time stand still. The woods also have a haunted reputation as people have seen glimpses of a figure between the trees.

It is very possible that the Tremayne family carried out licensed hangings in the garden in the 17th century and some believe that a tree bent over (Pengrugla) was in fact the gallows. Certainly there is a peculiar atmosphere nearby.

Finally, Heligan House, built in the early 17th century also fails to escape the ghostly reputation. It is said that doors often open and close by themselves and many people claim to have seen a lady dressed in Grey walking from the house, down a path (known as Grey Lady's Walk), across the lawn, before disappearing into the trees near the stables.

Can there be an explanation for these ghostly goings on and the melancholy atmosphere emanating throughout the gardens?

The history of the gardens in the 18th and 19th centuries and the Tremayne family estate before and during this time may offer some indications. However, some of the atmosphere may be levelled at the deaths which befell so many of it's gardeners during The Great War. Most of the workers died and ultimately this led to the gardens decline. Perhaps the impending sadness of these brave men has somehow remained.

Finally, it may be worth noting that a while ago an exorcist was called in to try and remove whatever may be at Heligan. A local vicar came and carried out a service which apparently did ease some of the extreme sadness. However, it does seem that much of the reported phenomenon remains at the Lost Gardens of Heligan.

ROCHE ROCK

On the moor, near the village of Roche, lies sinister Roche Rock, often cold even in summer. A strange edifice, believed to be a ruined 15th century chapel rises prominently from the summit of the rock. The chapel and the rocks themselves also have a ghoulish reputation. The infamous ghost of the Demon Tregeagle, famed throughout Cornwall for his ghostly shenanigans, is deemed to have once visited here whilst fleeing from his hellish pursuers. It is unlikely though that he explains the noises heard coming from the ruin or the other eerie experiences. Many people have seen a shadowy figure bending among the rocks or fleeing up them towards the top. A man has also been seen looking from a ruined window in the chapel. Yet when people have climbed the rocks they have found themselves to be completely alone. Some say this figure is a monk who lived here many centuries ago, others believe the figure to be a leper who hid away at Roche rock while disease overcame him and there are others who claim him to be a smuggler. Whatever the truth, we may never know!

PREVIOUS BOOK UPDATES

In my last book "Ghost Hunting..." there were several stories for which I have subsequently researched new information. I am sure many readers of this book will be very interested in such information. If you are, read on...

ST MARY'S CHURCH YARD

Since I wrote about this location, there have been several more sightings of the white figure, including two very interesting reports appearing in the Cornishman newspaper. On the 25th, May, 2000 the paper printed an article about a young man from Hayle who saw the figure at about 10.00pm one evening, that week and in February, 2001 they also printed a letter from a man who claimed that he and a friend also saw the figure, one night. I have also spoken to several other witnesses, who have claimed to see the figure and was also present with my wife and fifteen people on a Ghost Tour when something strange materialised in the church yard. We saw a strange spiral of 'mist', the shape of a person, floating above the ground, for several seconds. All those present witnessed this phenomenon, many becoming very scared. However, it was not the white figure in question and I am sure there may be a rational explanation (answers on a post card!).

Further to stories of figures in church yards, I have also learnt of yet another, in a cemetery in Cornwall...

LAUNCESTON CHURCH YARD

This church yard is believed to be haunted by a "Kergrim", a Cornish ghoul. It is described as an extremely unpleasant figure, spotted in several locations around the church yard. Like other cemetery figures, this is also believed to be some kind of guardian, watching over the deceased.

ANCIENT STONES

I have recently discovered several tales relating to the many ancient stones in West Cornwall. As I have already noted, it is believed that these places are haunted by long dead spirits. They are certainly very powerful places (just ask your local dowser) and I have found more evidence to support claims, that they are indeed home to some very peculiar figures.

CARN KENIDJACK: I previously wrote about the mysterious goings on at night at Kenidjack. Several people have since contacted me to tell me how they also find it a very unnerving place, particularly at night . It has an atmosphere all of it's own. For example I received a letter from a gentleman in London who said that although he doesn't frighten easily he believes there is an "air of eeriness" at Kenidjack, particularly at dusk.

TRENCROM: In the vicinity of Trencrom Hill, there was originally an Iron Age fort. Many strange incidents have occurred here, leading many to believe the place to be haunted, possibly by Iron Age tribes. In the 1960s four people were driving past Trencrom in a car when their car suddenly and inexplicably died. Looking around, they suddenly saw the strange figure of a man, he seemed to be staring at them from just a short distance away. To their amazement he just vanished. This was followed by something even more bizarre. The car suddenly and inexplicably restarted. They later had the car examined but could find nothing wrong. They immediately drove off at great speed, very scared by their experience. This, or similar, figure has been seen on several other occasions, always described as dark, with rough clothing. It is always in the same location and he always vanishes, soon after making his appearance. Also at this spot, strange 'bluish' lights have frequently been seen at night, dancing across the countryside, Jack Harry's lanterns?

Also on Trencrom Hill itself, there are claims that many people experience a very eerie feeling of being watched. Dogs have been known to become fearful, barking, growling, with their hackles rising. Several people claim that the area is haunted by

Iron Age soldiers, part of an ancient tribe, long deceased.

Other stones are said to be haunted by 'the lady of the vow'. This is said to be a beautiful lady dressed in white, carrying a red rose in her mouth. However, she suggests great trouble ahead for anyone who encounters her.

THE MERRY MAIDENS, near Lamorna, have several strange legends. One of which claims that several ghostly figures have been seen at night. Are they ghosts, or historic scenes recorded on the rocks themselves?

TREWITHEN LANE

I also wrote about the white lady who was seen in the lane leading to Trewithen Road, Penzance. It seems that there have been more experiences. One man tells me how he walks his dogs in the lane, frequently and there is one particular place where the dogs always start to act up. They always begin to act nervously and aggressively. Furthermore the atmosphere in this place can be "cut with a knife". The place is very eerie and is often pitch black and many other people feel extremely uneasy here. However, I have heard another story which is altogether more fascinating. A few months ago a young lady was walking down the lane, when she suddenly felt she was being followed. She kept looking around but could not see anybody. However, she still had a strong sense of a presence which seemed to be following at the same distance behind. She quickly sped through the lane and walked to her father-in law's house. Here she spoke of her strange experience, completely without knowledge of any similar tales about the lane. At this point her father-in-law gathered up his copy of my last book and showed her the story inside. She was amazed because she had no previous knowledge of any tale and was surprised at the similarity to her own experience.

KERRIS

Since writing about the horse heard at Kerris, I have been told several other interesting tales about the village. The manor house mentioned was a Tudor ruin rebuilt in the eighteenth century. In 1948 a man standing near the manor house saw a figure on horseback, which simply vanished in front of his eyes. The figure was wearing a great coat and a small fur hat. In 1968 a man walking on the same road also suddenly came across a rider and horse, meeting the same description. He believed the man to be an army officer from the early 19th century. However, the horse and man made no sound.

Then in 1970 a family who knew nothing of the story, or the area were camping nearby. At night they suddenly heard clear horses footsteps in a field, nearby. In the morning, no footprints were to be seen, but they were convinced they had heard horses hooves. The next night the wife awoke to similar noises. She quickly looked outside the tent and was surprised to see a man on horseback, speeding towards the tent. She threw herself over her children, for fear of being trampled but was amazed when nothing happened. She looked outside but the figure had vanished and the field was now empty. they were so terrified they immediately packed up their belongings and left.

KERRIS FARMHOUSE: Several years ago some people went to look at the farmhouse, with an estate agent, intending to buy it. The large, heavy, front door was left open while they toured inside. They immediately sensed an eerie feeling in the building and soon planned to make their excuses and leave. However, they suddenly discovered the front door had been shut, yet it seemed too heavy for the wind. As they tried to open it, it would not budge, as if someone was holding it. The three of them shoved it, with no success. Eventually they had to leave via the overgrown back entrance. They were pleased to leave, but left behind them an anxious estate agent , very nervous of staying there for the next prospective buyers, alone.

GHOST WALKS

If you are interested in visiting many haunted places on a ghost walk around the towns of Penzance and St Ives with the author. Please phone 01736 331206 or send an s.a.e. to Ghost Walks; 23 Pendennis Road, Penzance, TR18 2BA for more details.

PENGERSICK CASTLE

For anyone interested in spending a "ghost night" at Pengersick Castle contact the above details for more information. Such nights have proved to be very rewarding and it is hoped to continue running these in the future. Dare you spend some time at Pengersick?